REPENT

Apostle Bill Amor

REPENT
written by Bill Amor
1st Edition © 2025 by Bill Amor
ISBN 979-8-218-67749-7

Contents

CONTENTS

Step 1: Understanding the Theme of "Repent!"

The title "Repent!" suggests that Apostle Bill Amor's book will focus on the biblical concept of repentance, which is a central theme in Christian theology. To create a summary based on the Amplified Bible (AMP), we must explore key passages and teachings about repentance as described in the AMP Bible. These include its definition, importance, process, and outcomes.

Step 2: Key Biblical Passages on Repentance in the AMP Bible

The following passages from the AMP Bible provide foundational insights into repentance:

- **Acts 2:38**: Peter calls for repentance, baptism in Jesus' name for forgiveness of sins, and receiving the Holy Spirit.

- **Acts 3:19**: Repentance is tied to turning away from sin and experiencing spiritual refreshment.

- **Luke 15:7**: Heaven rejoices over one sinner who repents.

- **Mark 1:15**: Jesus begins His ministry with a call to repent and believe in the gospel.

- **Revelation 22** (general context): Emphasizes living righteously and being prepared for Christ's return.

These verses highlight that repentance involves a change of mind, turning away from sin, accepting God's forgiveness through Jesus Christ, and living a transformed life.

Step 3: Structuring the Summary

Using these biblical principles, we can summarize Apostle Bill Amor's book based on themes such as defining repentance, its necessity for salvation, its transformative power, and its eternal significance.

Summary of "Repent!" by Apostle Bill Amor

Apostle Bill Amor's upcoming book **"Repent!"** delves deeply into the biblical concept of repentance as presented in Scripture. Drawing extensively from the Amplified Bible (AMP), this work explores how repentance serves as a cornerstone of Christian faith and salvation. The book emphasizes that true repentance is not merely feeling regret or sorrow but involves a profound transformation of heart and mind—a complete turning away from sinful ways toward God.

The Call to Repentance

The book begins by examining Peter's powerful sermon in Acts 2:38 where he declares, "Repent [change your old way of thinking, turn from your sinful ways, accept and follow Jesus as the Messiah] and be baptized... because of the forgiveness of your sins; and you will receive the gift of the Holy Spirit." This foundational verse underscores that repentance is both an invitation and a command for all who seek reconciliation with God. It highlights how repentance leads to forgiveness through Jesus Christ and opens believers to receive God's Spirit.

The Process of Repentance

Apostle Amor explains that true repentance involves more than acknowledging wrongdoing — it requires an active decision to change one's behavior. Drawing from Mark 1:15 ("Repent [change your inner self—your old way of thinking], regret past sins, live your life in a way that proves repentance; seek God's purpose for your life"), he outlines practical steps for believers to align their lives with God's will. This includes confessing sins, seeking forgiveness through Christ's sacrifice, and committing to ongoing spiritual growth.

The Joyful Outcome

One key theme explored is how heaven rejoices when sinners repent (Luke 15:7). The author reflects on Jesus' parables about lost sheep and prodigal sons to illustrate God's immense love for those who turn back to Him. Repentance brings not only personal peace but also divine joy as it restores broken relationships between humanity and God.

Repentance as Preparation

In light of Revelation 22's message about Christ's imminent return ("Behold, I am coming quickly..."), Apostle Amor stresses that repentance prepares believers for eternal life. By washing their robes in righteousness (Revelation 22:14), Christians gain access to the tree of life—a symbol of eternal blessings with God. The book warns against delaying repentance since judgment is final (Revelation 22:11).

A Transformative Journey

Finally, "Repent!" emphasizes that repentance is not a one-time act but an ongoing journey marked by humility, obedience, and faithfulness. As Acts 3:19 states ("So repent [change your inner self—your old way of thinking], turn back [to God], so that your sins may be wiped away..."), Apostle Amor encourages readers to embrace daily renewal through prayer, Scripture study, and reliance on the Holy Spirit.

By weaving together scriptural insights with practical applications, Apostle Bill Amor's "Repent!" serves as both a theological guidebook and an inspirational call-to-action for believers seeking deeper intimacy with God. Through heartfelt reflection on biblical truths found in passages like Acts 2:38–47 and Revelation 22, this book reminds readers that genuine repentance leads not only to forgiveness but also to spiritual transformation—and ultimately eternal life with Christ.

Introduction to "Repent!" by Apostle Bill Amor

A Call to Transformation

"Repent!"—a single word that echoes through centuries of divine revelation, calling humanity back into alignment with God's perfect will. In this book, Apostle Bill Amor invites readers on a profound journey into one of Scripture's most urgent commands: **repentance.** Rooted in the timeless truths of the Amplified Bible (AMP), this work explores what it means to truly repent—to change your inner self, abandon sinful ways, and seek God's purpose for your life.

From John the Baptist's cry in Matthew 3:2—"Repent [change your inner self—your old way of thinking; regret past sins], for the kingdom of heaven is at hand"—to Peter's powerful sermon in Acts 2:38—"Repent [change your old way of thinking]...and you will receive the gift of the Holy Spirit"—the message remains clear and unchanging. Repentance is not merely an act; it is a transformation that begins within and manifests outwardly in obedience and faithfulness.

The Urgency of Repentance

Throughout Scripture, God repeatedly calls His people to turn back to Him. In Zechariah 1:3, He declares, "Return to Me...and I shall return to you." This divine invitation reveals both God's justice and His mercy—a reminder that while sin separates us from Him, repentance restores our fellowship with Him. Similarly, Revelation 2:4-5 warns believers against losing their first love for God but offers hope through repentance: "Remember...repent [change your inner self—your old way of thinking]...and do the works you did at first."

A Journey Toward Renewal

This book seeks to illuminate how repentance serves as both a starting point and a continual practice in every believer's walk with Christ. It challenges readers not only to acknowledge their shortcomings but also to embrace God's grace and power for lasting change. As Peter proclaimed on Pentecost (Acts 2), repentance opens the door to forgiveness, renewal, and empowerment by the Holy Spirit.

Apostle Bill Amor writes with urgency because he understands that repentance is not optional—it is essential. Whether you are encountering this call for the first time or returning after wandering far from God's path, "Repent!" offers guidance rooted in Scripture and inspired by God's enduring love.

An Invitation

As you read this book, let these words resonate deeply within your heart: "Repent [change your inner self—your old way of thinking]...forgiveness awaits." May this journey lead you closer to God's presence and purpose for your life.

Chapters for "Repent!"

Chapter 1: What Is Repentance?

This chapter will define repentance from a biblical perspective. It will explore the original meanings of the term in Hebrew ("teshuvah") and Greek ("metanoia"), emphasizing its significance as a change of heart and mind rather than mere regret or guilt. The chapter will also discuss how repentance is central to Christian faith.

Chapter 2: Why Repentance Matters

This chapter will delve into why repentance is essential for spiritual growth and salvation. It will explain how sin separates humanity from God and how repentance restores that relationship. Biblical passages like Acts 3:19 ("Repent therefore, and turn back...") can be used to illustrate this point.

Chapter 3: The Process of True Repentance

Here, readers will learn about the steps involved in genuine repentance—acknowledging sin, feeling godly sorrow (as opposed to worldly sorrow), confessing sins to God, seeking forgiveness, and turning away from sinful behavior. This chapter could include practical exercises for self-reflection.

Chapter 4: Biblical Examples of Repentance

This chapter will highlight stories from Scripture that demonstrate true repentance. Examples may include King David's confession after his sin with Bathsheba (Psalm 51), the Prodigal Son (Luke 15), and Nineveh's collective repentance in response to Jonah's warning (Jonah 3).

Chapter 5: Common Misconceptions About Repentance

This chapter will address misunderstandings such as thinking that repentance is a one-time act or equating it with perfectionism. It will clarify that repentance is an ongoing process of transformation through God's grace.

Chapter 6: The Role of Grace in Repentance

This section will focus on how God's grace empowers believers to repent. It will emphasize that while humans are called to repent, it is ultimately God's Spirit that enables true change (Ephesians 2:8-9). This chapter can also discuss how grace prevents legalism or self-condemnation during the process.

Chapter 7: Daily Repentance as a Lifestyle

Building on earlier chapters, this section will encourage readers to make daily introspection and self-improvement part of their spiritual routine.

Chapter 8: The Fruits of Repentance

The final chapter will explore the transformative power of repentance—how it leads to peace with God, personal growth, restored relationships, and greater joy in life. Using Galatians 5:22-23 (the fruits of the Spirit) as a framework, this chapter can inspire readers by showing them what lies on the other side of sincere repentance

Chapter 1: What Is Repentance?

Introduction to Repentance

Repentance is a concept that lies at the very heart of the Christian faith. It is a term often heard in sermons, read in Scripture, and discussed in theological circles. However, its true meaning is sometimes misunderstood or reduced to feelings of guilt or regret. To fully grasp repentance from a biblical perspective, it is essential to explore its original meanings in both Hebrew and Greek—the languages in which the Bible was originally written. These linguistic roots reveal that repentance is far more profound than mere sorrow for wrongdoing; it signifies a transformative change of heart, mind, and direction.

In this chapter, we will delve into the biblical definitions of repentance as expressed through the Hebrew word "teshuvah" and the Greek word "metanoia." We will also examine how repentance functions as a cornerstone of Christian theology and practice.

The Hebrew Concept of Repentance: Teshuvah

The Hebrew word for repentance, **"teshuvah" (הבושת),** carries a rich and multifaceted meaning. Derived from the root verb "shuv," which means "to return," teshuvah literally translates to "returning." In its biblical context, teshuvah refers to turning away from sin and returning to God with one's whole being—physically, emotionally, and spiritually.

Unlike modern interpretations that often equate repentance with guilt or remorse alone, teshuvah emphasizes action. It involves recognizing one's departure from God's ways and making an intentional decision to realign oneself with Him. This process is not merely about feeling sorry but about actively choosing to turn back toward righteousness.

For example, in Joel 2:12-13, God calls His people to return (teshuvah) with all their hearts:
"Even now," declares the LORD, "return to me with all your heart, with fasting and weeping and mourning. Rend your heart and not your garments."
This passage highlights that true repentance goes beyond outward displays of sorrow; it requires an inward transformation—a heartfelt commitment to seek God.

In Jewish thought, teshuvah is seen as a continuous journey rather than a one-time event. It involves ongoing self-reflection, confession of sins, seeking forgiveness from those wronged (as well as from God), and striving for personal growth. The ultimate goal of teshuvah is reconciliation with God—a restoration of the relationship between humanity and its Creator.

The Greek Concept of Repentance: Metanoia

In the New Testament, the Greek word most commonly translated as repentance is **"metanoia" (μετάνοια)**. This term provides another layer of understanding by focusing on an internal transformation—a change in one's mind or way of thinking.

Etymologically, metanoia combines two Greek words:

- **Meta**, meaning "after" or "beyond,"

- **Noeo**, meaning "to think" or "to perceive."

Together, metanoia conveys the idea of rethinking or re-considering one's life in light of divine truth. It represents a radical shift in perspective—a complete reorientation of priorities that aligns one's thoughts and values with God's will.

Metanoia appears frequently throughout Jesus' teachings in the Gospels. For instance:
"Repent (metanoeite), for the kingdom of heaven has come near." (Matthew 4:17)
Here Jesus calls His listeners not just to feel remorse but to undergo a profound transformation—to abandon their old ways of thinking and embrace God's kingdom.

It is important to note that metanoia does not end with intellectual acknowledgment; it leads to tangible changes in behavior. As theologian Richard Trench described it: *"A mighty change of mind, heart, and life that can only be brought about by the Spirit of God."*

Repentance as Central to Christian Faith

Both teshuvah and metanoia underscore that repentance is far more than regret or guilt—it is an active process involving both inner transformation and outward action. This dual nature makes repentance foundational within Christianity.

Repentance as Turning Toward God

At its core, repentance involves turning away from sin—anything that separates us from God—and turning toward Him instead. This act requires humility: acknowledging our need for forgiveness while trusting in God's grace.

The parable of the prodigal son (Luke 15:11-32) beautifully illustrates this concept. The younger son recognizes his wrongdoing ("I have sinned against heaven"), turns away from his sinful lifestyle ("he got up"), and returns home seeking reconciliation with his father. The father's joyful welcome demonstrates God's readiness to forgive those who repent sincerely.

Repentance Leads to Transformation

True repentance results in lasting change—not just temporary remorse but genuine transformation empowered by God's Spirit (Romans 12:2). As believers experience this renewal daily through prayerful reflection on Scripture—and through reliance on Christ—they grow closer in their walk with Him.

Repentance Opens the Door to Salvation

Finally—and most importantly—repentance plays an essential role in salvation itself. Acts 3:19 declares: *"Repent then and turn back so that your sins may be wiped out."* Without repentance there can be no forgiveness; without forgiveness there can be no reconciliation with God.

Conclusion

Repentance, when understood through its biblical roots—
teshuvah («return») and **metanoia** («change of mind»)—is
revealed as much more than mere regret or sorrow over
sin. It encompasses an active decision to turn away from
sinfulness while embracing God›s truth wholeheartedly. This
process transforms both our inner selves (our hearts/minds)
and our outward actions (our lives).

As Christians embark on this journey daily—with faith guid-
ing each step—they draw closer into fellowship with their
Creator while reflecting His image more fully within themselves.

In subsequent chapters we will explore practical aspects
surrounding how believers can cultivate authentic repentance within their lives—but first let us remember this foundational truth: Repentance begins not simply by looking
backward at past mistakes but by looking forward toward
God's redemptive grace!

Chapter 2: Why Repentance Matters

Understanding the Importance of Repentance

Repentance is not merely a religious ritual or an abstract concept; it is a transformative process that lies at the heart of spiritual growth and salvation. To understand why repentance matters, we must first explore the nature of sin and its consequences. Sin creates a barrier between humanity and God, disrupting the relationship He intended for us to have with Him. Repentance serves as the bridge that restores this broken connection, allowing us to experience God's grace, forgiveness, and renewal.

In Acts 3:19, Peter calls on his audience to repent: **"Repent therefore, and turn back, that your sins may be blotted out."** This verse encapsulates the essence of repentance— it is a turning away from sin and a turning toward God. Without repentance, there can be no reconciliation with God or true spiritual transformation.

Sin as Separation from God

The Bible teaches that sin separates humanity from God. In Isaiah 59:2, it states: **"But your iniquities have made a separation between you and your God, and your sins have hidden His face from you so that He does not hear."** This separation is not merely metaphorical; it represents a profound spiritual chasm caused by disobedience to God's will. Sin alienates us from God's holiness and disrupts our ability to live in harmony with Him.

This separation has eternal consequences. Romans 6:23 warns: **"For the wages of sin is death, but the free gift of God is eternal life in Christ Jesus our Lord."** The "death" referred to here is both physical and spiritual—a complete estrangement from God's presence. However, through repentance, we are offered a way back into fellowship with Him.

Repentance Restores Our Relationship with God

Repentance is essential because it allows us to reconcile with God. When we repent, we acknowledge our wrong-doing and express genuine sorrow for our sins. But repentance goes beyond mere regret—it involves a change of mind (the Greek word for repentance, *metanoia*, literally means "a change of mind") and a commitment to turn away from sinful behavior.

David's prayer in Psalm 51 provides a powerful example of repentance leading to restoration. After committing grievous sins—adultery with Bathsheba and orchestrating her husband's death—David cried out to God: **"Create in me a clean heart, O God, and renew a right spirit within me" (Psalm 51:10).** David›s heartfelt plea demonstrates that true repentance leads to forgiveness and renewal.

God's response to genuine repentance is always one of mercy and grace. Joel 2:13 reminds us: **"Return to the Lord your God, for He is gracious and merciful, slow to anger, and abounding in steadfast love; and He relents over disaster."** Through repentance, we are not only forgiven but also restored into right standing with God.

Repentance as an Act of Faith

Repentance is inseparable from faith—it requires believing in God's promises of forgiveness through Jesus Christ. In Mark 1:15, Jesus begins His ministry by proclaiming: **"The time is fulfilled, and the kingdom of God is at hand; repent and believe in the gospel."** Here we see that repentance involves both turning away from sin and turning toward faith in Christ.

Faith without repentance is incomplete because it fails to address the root problem—our rebellion against God's authority. Similarly, repentance without faith lacks direction; it becomes an empty exercise unless accompanied by trust in Jesus' redemptive work on the cross.

Acts 20:21 emphasizes this dual aspect when Paul declares his message was about **"repentance toward God and faith in our Lord Jesus Christ."** Together, these two elements form the foundation for salvation.

The Fruits of True Repentance

True repentance produces tangible results—a transformed life marked by obedience to God's will. John the Baptist emphasized this when he said: **"Bear fruit in keeping with repentance" (Matthew 3:8).** Genuine repentance leads to visible changes in behavior as we align ourselves more closely with Gods standards.

One striking biblical example is Zacchaeus' encounter with Jesus (Luke 19). As a tax collector who had defrauded others for personal gain, Zacchaeus demonstrated true repentance by declaring: **"Behold, Lord, half of my goods I give to the poor. And if I have defrauded anyone of anything, I restore it fourfold" (Luke 19:8).** His actions reflected his changed heart—a hallmark of authentic repentance.

Paul echoes this idea in Acts 26:20 when he describes his ministry as calling people **"to repent and turn to God, performing deeds in keeping with their repentance."** These deeds are not what save us but are evidence that our hearts have been genuinely transformed by God›s grace.

Why Repentance Is Necessary for Salvation

At its core, salvation requires acknowledging our need for forgiveness—a recognition that comes through repentance. Jesus Himself declared: **"Unless you repent, you will all likewise perish" (Luke 13:3).** This stark warning underscores how critical repentance is for avoiding spiritual destruction.

Repentance also opens the door for receiving God's gift of salvation through Christ's sacrifice on the cross. As Peter preached on Pentecost Day: **"Repent and be baptized every one of you in the name of Jesus Christ for the forgiveness of your sins..." (Acts 2:38).** Through this act of turning away from sin toward faith in Christ›s atonement, we receive not only forgiveness but also new life empowered by the Holy Spirit.

Conclusion

Repentance matters because it addresses humanity's greatest problem—separation from God due to sin—and offers reconciliation through His grace. It restores our relationship with Him while producing lasting transformation evidenced by changed lives. Without genuine repentance paired with faith in Christ's redemptive work on Calvary's cross, there can be no true salvation or spiritual growth.

As Acts 3:19 reminds us once again: **"Repent therefore, and turn back—that your sins may be blotted out."** Let this call resonate deeply within us as we seek daily renewal through heartfelt confession before our loving Creator who stands ready always—to forgive abundantly those who return humbly unto Him!

Chapter 3: The Process of True Repentance

Repentance is a transformative process that allows individuals to turn away from sin and align themselves with God's will. It is not merely a checklist of actions but a heartfelt journey toward spiritual renewal and reconciliation with God. This chapter outlines the essential steps involved in genuine repentance, emphasizing the importance of self-reflection, godly sorrow, confession, seeking forgiveness, and forsaking sinful behavior. Practical exercises are also included to help readers internalize these principles.

Acknowledging Sin

The first step in true repentance is recognizing and admitting one's sins. This requires honest self-reflection and humility. Sin can manifest as transgressions against God's commandments, harmful actions toward others, or even neglecting righteous duties. Acknowledging sin means taking full responsibility for one's actions without excuses or justifications.

Practical Exercise: Self-Reflection Journal

- Set aside time each day to reflect on your thoughts, words, and actions.

- Write down instances where you may have fallen short of God's commandments.

- Ask yourself: "Have I harmed others through my actions? Have I neglected opportunities to do good?"

This exercise helps cultivate awareness of personal short-comings and prepares the heart for the next steps in repentance.

Feeling Godly Sorrow

True repentance involves experiencing *godly sorrow*, which is distinct from worldly sorrow. Worldly sorrow often arises from fear of consequences or regret over being caught. In contrast, godly sorrow stems from a deep realization that one's sins have offended God and caused harm to oneself and others. It is a heartfelt remorse that leads to a sincere desire for change.

Scriptural Insight

The Apostle Paul explains this concept in 2 Corinthians 7:10: "For godly sorrow worketh repentance to salvation not to be repented of: but the sorrow of the world worketh death."

Practical Exercise: Prayerful Reflection

- Pray earnestly to God, asking Him to help you feel genuine remorse for your sins.

- Meditate on how your actions have affected your relationship with God and others.

- Reflect on Christ's atoning sacrifice and how your sins contributed to His suffering.

This practice fosters humility and opens the heart to divine guidance.

Confessing Sins

Confession is an essential part of repentance. It involves openly acknowledging sins before God through sincere prayer. For serious transgressions, confession may also require speaking with a trusted spiritual leader (such as a bishop or pastor) who can provide guidance and support.

Steps for Confession

1. Approach God in prayer with a humble heart.

2. Be specific about your sins—avoid vague generalities.

3. Express genuine remorse and a desire for forgiveness.

Practical Exercise: Writing a Confession Prayer

- Write out a prayer confessing specific sins you've identified.

- Include expressions of remorse and gratitude for Christ's atonement.

- End by asking for strength to overcome temptations in the future.

This written exercise can serve as a starting point for verbal prayers or discussions with spiritual leaders.

Seeking Forgiveness

After confessing sins, it is crucial to seek forgiveness—not only from God but also from those who may have been hurt by your actions. Seeking forgiveness demonstrates humility and a willingness to make amends.

Steps for Seeking Forgiveness

1. Pray sincerely for God's mercy and grace.

2. Approach those you've wronged with humility; apologize without justifying your actions.

3. Be prepared to listen if they express their feelings about how they were affected.

Practical Exercise: Forgiveness Outreach Plan

- Make a list of people you may have wronged.

- Plan how you will approach each person—consider writing letters if face-to-face conversations are difficult.

- Pray for courage before reaching out.

This exercise encourages accountability while fostering healing relationships.

Turning Away from Sinful Behavior (Forsaking Sin)

True repentance requires more than feeling sorry—it demands action. Forsaking sin means making deliberate efforts to avoid repeating past mistakes by changing behaviors, attitudes, and environments that lead to temptation.

Steps for Forsaking Sin

1. Identify triggers or circumstances that lead you into sin.

2. Replace sinful habits with righteous ones (e.g., replace gossiping with uplifting conversations).

3. Seek support from trusted friends or mentors who can hold you accountable.

Practical Exercise: Habit Replacement Plan

- Identify one recurring sin in your life (e.g., dishonesty).

- Write down specific ways you will avoid situations that lead to this sin (e.g., committing beforehand always to tell the truth).

- List positive habits or activities that can replace sinful behaviors (e.g., practicing honesty even in small matters).

By actively forsaking sin, individuals demonstrate their commitment to living righteously moving forward.

Conclusion: The Transformative Power of Repentance

Repentance is not an event but an ongoing process—a journey toward becoming more Christlike each day. As individuals acknowledge their sins, feel godly sorrow, confess their wrongdoings, seek forgiveness, and forsake sinful behavior, they experience profound spiritual growth and renewal.

The Savior Himself stands ready to assist us every step of the way: "Come unto me all ye that labour and are heavy laden, and I will give you rest" (Matthew 11:28). Through His atoning sacrifice, we are empowered not only to repent but also to find lasting peace and joy in His grace.

Let this chapter serve as both a guidebook for personal transformation and an invitation to embrace the Savior's infinite love through true repentance.

"Yet forty days, and Nineveh shall be overthrown!" (Jonah 3:4)

Initially reluctant but eventually obedient after being swallowed by a great fish (Jonah 1-2), Jonah delivered this warning throughout the city. Remarkably, the people believed Jonah's message without hesitation:

"The people of Nineveh believed God; they proclaimed a fast and put on sackcloth—from the greatest of them even unto the least." (Jonah 3:5)

Even the king humbled himself by removing his royal robes, covering himself in sackcloth, sitting in ashes—a traditional sign of mourning—and issuing a decree urging everyone in

Nineveh:

"Let everyone call urgently on God! Let them give up their evil ways..." (Jonah 3:8)

Their actions demonstrated genuine repentance through fasting, prayer, humility before God, and turning away from violence and wickedness. In response to their sincerity:

"When God saw what they did—how they turned from their evil ways—He relented from bringing upon them the destruction He had threatened." (Jonah 3:10)

Nineveh's story highlights several important truths about repentance:

1. **Urgency** – The people responded immediately upon hearing God›s warning.

2. **Humility** – Both leaders and common citizens humbled themselves before God.

3. **Transformation** – True repentance led them not only to seek forgiveness but also change their behavior.

This account underscores God's willingness to extend mercy even toward those who seem beyond redemption if they sincerely turn back toward Him.

Chapter 4: Biblical Examples of Repentance

Repentance is a central theme throughout the Bible, and Scripture provides numerous examples of individuals and groups who turned away from sin and sought reconciliation with God. These stories not only illustrate the transformative power of repentance but also highlight God's mercy and readiness to forgive those who genuinely repent. In this chapter, we will explore three significant biblical examples of repentance: King David's confession after his sin with Bathsheba, the Prodigal Son's return to his father, and Nineveh's collective repentance in response to Jonah's warning.

King David's Confession After His Sin with Bathsheba (Psalm 51)

King David's story is one of the most profound examples of personal repentance in the Bible. As recorded in 2 Samuel 11-12, David committed adultery with Bathsheba, the wife of Uriah, and then orchestrated Uriah's death to cover up his sin. For a time, David attempted to continue his life as though nothing had happened. However, God sent the prophet Nathan to confront him with a parable that exposed his guilt. When Nathan declared, "You are the man!" (2 Samuel 12:7), David was struck by the weight of his wrongdoing.

David's response was one of deep remorse and genuine repentance. He did not attempt to justify or minimize his actions but instead acknowledged his sin before God. Psalm 51 captures David's heartfelt plea for forgiveness:

"Have mercy on me, O God, according to Your loving devotion; according to Your great compassion, blot out my transgressions. Wash me clean from my iniquity and cleanse me from my sin." (Psalm 51:1-2)

In this psalm, David expresses sorrow for his sins and asks God for a clean heart and renewed spirit. He recognizes that true repentance involves more than outward rituals; it requires a broken and contrite heart (Psalm 51:17). Although David faced consequences for his actions—such as the death of the child born from his affair—his sincere repentance restored his relationship with God.

David's story demonstrates that no sin is too great for God's forgiveness when approached with humility and genuine remorse.

The Prodigal Son (Luke 15)

The parable of the Prodigal Son is one of Jesus' most well-known teachings on repentance. Found in Luke 15:11-32, this story tells of a younger son who demands his inheritance from his father and then squanders it on reckless living in a distant country. When famine strikes and he finds himself destitute—longing even for the food given to pigs—the son comes to a realization:

"How many hired servants of my father have bread enough and to spare, and I perish with hunger! I will arise and go to my father..." (Luke 15:17-18)

The son decides to return home, fully prepared to confess his sins and ask only for a servant's position in his father's household. However, while he is still far off, his father sees him coming and runs to embrace him—a powerful image of God's love for repentant sinners.

The son confesses: *"Father, I have sinned against heaven and before you; I am no longer worthy to be called your son"* (Luke 15:21). But instead of rebuking him or treating him as a servant, the father restores him as a beloved son by clothing him in fine garments and celebrating with a feast.

This parable emphasizes several key aspects of repentance:

1. **Acknowledgment of Sin** – The son recognizes that he has sinned against both heaven (God) and his earthly father.

2. **Turning Back** – True repentance involves not just regret but action—a decision to return home.

3. **God's Mercy** – The father's joyful reception illustrates how eagerly God forgives those who turn back to Him.

Through this story, Jesus teaches that no matter how far someone has strayed or how unworthy they feel, God welcomes them back with open arms when they repent.

Nineveh's Collective Repentance (Jonah 3)

The city of Nineveh provides an extraordinary example of collective repentance on a massive scale. As described in Jonah 3, God commanded Jonah to deliver a message warning Nineveh—a notoriously wicked city—that its destruction was imminent due to its sins:

"Yet forty days, and Nineveh shall be overthrown!" (Jonah 3:4)

Initially reluctant but eventually obedient after being swallowed by a great fish (Jonah 1-2), Jonah delivered this warning throughout the city. Remarkably, the people believed Jonah's message without hesitation:

"The people of Nineveh believed God; they proclaimed a fast and put on sackcloth—from the greatest of them even unto the least." (Jonah 3:5)

Even the king humbled himself by removing his royal robes, covering himself in sackcloth, sitting in ashes—a traditional sign of mourning—and issuing a decree urging everyone in Nineveh:

"Let everyone call urgently on God! Let them give up their evil ways..." (Jonah 3:8)

Their actions demonstrated genuine repentance through

fasting, prayer, humility before God, and turning away from violence and wickedness. In response to their sincerity:

"When God saw what they did—how they turned from their evil ways—He relented from bringing upon them the destruction He had threatened." (Jonah 3:10)

Nineveh's story highlights several important truths about repentance:

1. **Urgency** – The people responded immediately upon hearing God›s warning.

2. **Humility** – Both leaders and common citizens humbled themselves before God.

3. **Transformation** – True repentance led them not only to seek forgiveness but also change their behavior.

This account underscores God's willingness to extend mercy even toward those who seem beyond redemption if they sincerely turn back toward Him.

Conclusion

These biblical examples vividly illustrate what true repentance looks like—whether it is an individual like King David pouring out their heart before God after personal failure; someone like the Prodigal Son making an active decision to return home after straying far away; or an entire city like Nineveh humbling itself collectively before God's judgment.

Each story reveals key elements:

1. Acknowledgment of wrongdoing.

2. Genuine sorrow over sin.

3. A decisive turning away from sinful behavior toward obedience.

4. Trusting fully in God's mercy rather than relying on human merit.

Above all else these accounts remind us that **repentance opens wide the door for restoration**, allowing individuals—and even entire communities—to experience God's boundless grace when they turn back toward Him wholeheartedly.

Chapter 5: Common Misconceptions About Repentance

Repentance is a central theme in the Christian faith, yet it is often misunderstood or misrepresented. Many believers and non-believers alike hold misconceptions about what repentance truly entails. In this chapter, we will address some of the most common misunderstandings about repentance, such as the belief that it is a one-time act or that it equates to achieving perfectionism. We will also clarify how repentance is an ongoing process of transformation through God's grace.

Repentance Is Not a One-Time Act

One of the most prevalent misconceptions about repentance is that it is a single event—something that happens once when someone first comes to faith in Christ. While initial repentance, often referred to as "repentance unto salvation," marks an important turning point in a believer's life, **true biblical repentance is not confined to a single moment but is instead an ongoing process throughout the Christian journey**.

The Greek word for repentance, *metanoia,* means "a change of mind." This change of mind involves not only turning away from sin but also continually aligning oneself with God's will. Jesus Himself emphasized this when He began His ministry by proclaiming, "Repent and believe the good news" (Mark 1:15). The verbs used here are in the present imperative tense, which implies continuous action—"be repenting and be believing."[1]

Martin Luther echoed this idea in his famous Ninety-Five Theses when he wrote: "When our Lord and Master Jesus Christ said 'Repent,' He willed the entire life of believers to be one of repentance."[2] This means that repentance does not end at conversion; rather, it becomes a lifelong practice as we grow in our relationship with God.

Even after salvation, Christians continue to struggle with sin because they live in fallen bodies within a broken world (Romans 7:18-25). As such, **daily repentance becomes essential for maintaining fellowship with God and allowing His sanctifying work to transform us**. Scripture supports this ongoing nature of repentance:

- In 1 John 1:9, believers are encouraged to confess their sins regularly: "If we confess our sins, He is faithful and just to forgive us our sins and cleanse us from all unrighteousness."

- Revelation 2:5 records Jesus calling the church at Ephesus to repent even after they had already come to faith: "Remember therefore from where you have fallen; repent and do the works you did at first."

Thus, far from being a one-time act, **repentance is an integral part of daily Christian living—a continual turning back toward God whenever we stray**.

Repentance Does Not Equal Perfectionism

Another common misunderstanding about repentance is equating it with perfectionism—the idea that true repentance requires achieving moral flawlessness or never sinning again. This misconception can lead to feelings of guilt or inadequacy when believers inevitably fall short. However, **biblical repentance does not demand perfection but rather genuine humility and reliance on God's grace.**

The Bible makes it clear that even faithful followers of Christ will stumble:

- Proverbs 24:16 says, "For though the righteous fall seven times, they rise again."

- The Apostle John reminds us in 1 John 1:8 that "if we say we have no sin, we deceive ourselves."

True repentance involves acknowledging our sins before God and seeking His forgiveness—not striving for unattainable perfection through human effort. As J.C. Ryle wisely stated: "The tears of repentance wash away no sins. That is the office...of the blood of Christ alone."[3] In other words, **it is Christ's sacrifice on the cross—not our own efforts—that secures forgiveness for our sins.**

Moreover, genuine repentance leads to transformation over time through the work of the Holy Spirit. Paul describes this process as being "transformed by the renewing of your mind" (Romans 12:2). This transformation does not happen overnight; rather, it unfolds gradually as believers submit themselves to God's sanctifying power.

It's important for Christians to remember that **repentance is not about achieving perfection but about pursuing holiness out of love for God.** When we repent sincerely and turn back toward Him after falling into sin, He graciously restores us and empowers us to live according to His will.

Repentance Is Rooted in Grace

A third misconception about repentance is viewing it as something we must do on our own strength or as a way to earn forgiveness from God. This misunderstanding can lead people either into despair—believing their efforts are never enough—or into pride—thinking they can achieve righteousness apart from God's help.

In reality, **repentance itself is a gift from God**, made possible by His grace working within us:

- Acts 11:18 speaks of how "God has granted even the Gentiles repentance unto life."

- James 1:18 reminds us that salvation comes entirely by God's initiative: "By His own choice He gave us birth by the word of truth."

Because true repentance flows from God's grace rather than human effort alone, Christians can approach Him confidently without fear that their confession must be "good enough" or "complete enough" to merit forgiveness.[4] Instead of relying on their own strength or sincerity as prerequisites for receiving mercy from Him who freely gives all things (Romans 8:32), believers rest securely knowing they are forgiven because Christ has already paid their debt fully at Calvary (Colossians 2:13-14).

This understanding frees Christians from both legalism (trying harder) and license (giving up altogether), enabling them instead simply to trust wholly upon Jesus' finished work while continuing to strive to grow closer Him each day through Spirit-led obedience rooted gratitude love.[5]

Conclusion

In summary:

1. Repentance isn't limited single moment conversion—its lifelong practice turning back toward whenever stray path righteousness
2. Doesn't require flawless behavior impossible attain fallen humanity instead calls humble submission dependence divine mercy
3. Ultimately rooted gracious gift bestowed sovereign Creator enables hearts minds transformed likeness Son

By dispelling these common misconceptions embracing fuller richer understanding biblical teaching regarding role importance lives believers alike better equipped walk faith-fully accordance purposes plans glory!

Chapter 6: The Role of Grace in Repentance

Introduction: Understanding Grace in the Context of Repentance

Repentance is a central theme in the Christian faith, calling believers to turn away from sin and align their lives with God's will. However, this process is not something humans can accomplish through sheer willpower or effort. Instead, repentance is deeply intertwined with the grace of God. As Ephesians 2:8-9 states, "For it is by grace you have been saved, through faith—and this is not from yourselves, it is the gift of God—not by works, so that no one can boast." This chapter explores how God's grace empowers believers to repent and how it prevents legalism or self-condemnation during the journey of transformation.

The Nature of Grace: A Divine Gift

Grace, by definition, is unmerited favor—a gift freely given by God to humanity despite our unworthiness. It is through this grace that believers are drawn to repentance. Without God's intervention and kindness, humans would remain trapped in sin. Romans 2:4 reminds us that it is "God's kindness [that] leads you toward repentance." This underscores that repentance begins not with human initiative but with God extending His grace to sinners.

God's grace does not merely forgive sins; it also transforms hearts. It enables individuals to see their need for change and gives them the strength to turn away from sin. Left to their own devices, people are incapable of achieving true repentance because sin blinds and enslaves them (John 8:34). Grace breaks these chains and opens the path toward reconciliation with God.

The Role of the Holy Spirit in Empowering Repentance

The Holy Spirit plays a critical role in applying God's grace to the believer's life. Jesus promised His followers that the Spirit would convict the world concerning sin, righteousness, and judgment (John 16:8). This conviction is an act of grace—it awakens individuals to their spiritual condition and points them toward Christ as their Savior.

Moreover, the Holy Spirit empowers believers to overcome sinful habits and live in obedience to God. Philippians 2:13 explains that "it is God who works in you to will and to act in order to fulfill his good purpose." This means that even the desire to repent comes from God's Spirit working within us. True change happens when we rely on His power rather than our own efforts.

Grace as a Guard Against Legalism

One of the dangers Christians face when pursuing repentance is falling into legalism—the belief that salvation or spiritual growth depends on human effort or adherence to rules. Legalism shifts focus away from God's grace and places undue emphasis on personal performance. This mindset leads either to pride (when one believes they are succeeding) or despair (when one feels they are failing).

Ephesians 2:8-9 directly counters legalistic thinking by affirming that salvation—and by extension, repentance—is a gift from God, not something earned through works. Recognizing this truth frees believers from striving for perfection out of fear or obligation. Instead, they can approach repentance with humility and gratitude for what Christ has already accomplished on their behalf.

Grace also reminds us that failure does not disqualify us from God's love or forgiveness. Proverbs 24:16 says, "Though a righteous man falls seven times, he rises again." Because of grace, believers can rise after every fall without fear of condemnation (Romans 8:1). This assurance encourages perseverance in repentance rather than giving up when struggles arise.

Grace as a Remedy for Self-Condemnation

Another challenge Christians may encounter during repentance is self-condemnation—a sense of unworthiness or shame over past sins. While conviction from the Holy Spirit leads us toward hope and restoration, self-condemnation traps us in guilt and despair.

Grace provides a remedy for this destructive mindset by reminding us that our worth comes not from our actions but from Christ's sacrifice on our behalf (Titus 3:5). When we understand that we are fully forgiven through His blood (1 John 1:9), we can let go of shame and embrace God's love.

Furthermore, grace teaches us patience with ourselves as we grow spiritually. Sanctification—the process of becoming more like Christ—is gradual and often involves setbacks. Rather than condemning ourselves for imperfections, we can trust that "he who began a good work in [us] will carry it on to completion until the day of Christ Jesus" (Philippians 1:6).

Living Out Repentance Through Grace

While repentance begins with God's grace, it also requires a response from us—faith expressed through action (James 2:17). However, even our ability to respond comes from God's enabling power. As Paul writes in Galatians 2:20, "I have been crucified with Christ and I no longer live, but Christ lives in me."

Living out repentance means continually relying on God's grace rather than trying harder on our own strength. It involves daily surrendering our will to Him and allowing His Spirit to guide our thoughts and actions (Romans 12:1-2). By doing so, we reflect His character more fully and bring glory to His name.

Conclusion: Gratitude for Grace

In summary, **grace lies at the heart of true repentance**—it initiates change within us through conviction by the Holy Spirit; it empowers us to overcome sin; it guards against legalism; it frees us from self-condemnation; and it sustains us as we grow closer to Christ each day.

As recipients of such an incredible gift, our response should be one of gratitude and humility. Rather than boasting about our efforts or achievements (Ephesians 2:9), let us boast only in what God has done for us through Jesus Christ (2 Corinthians 10:17). May His amazing grace continue transforming lives as we walk faithfully with

Chapter 7: Daily Repentance as a Lifestyle

Introduction: The Call to Daily Renewal

Repentance is often misunderstood as a one-time act or an event reserved for moments of grave mistakes. However, repentance is much more than that—it is a lifestyle, a daily practice of introspection and renewal that aligns us with our spiritual purpose. This chapter builds on the foundation laid in earlier sections by exploring how daily repentance can transform not only our relationship with God but also our personal growth and interactions with others.

The concept of daily repentance is rooted in humility and self-awareness. It requires acknowledging our imperfections, taking responsibility for our actions, and seeking forgiveness while committing to change. As Martin Luther famously stated in his first thesis of the 95 Theses: "When our Lord and Master Jesus Christ said, 'Repent,' He willed the entire life of believers to be one of repentance." This chapter will guide readers on how to integrate this principle into their everyday lives.

Understanding Repentance as a Process

Repentance is not merely about feeling regret or guilt; it is an ongoing process that involves reflection, confession, and transformation. In its original Greek form, the word "repent" (metanoeo) means "to change one's mind"—a profound shift in perspective that impacts how we think, act, and live.

Daily repentance begins with recognizing that sin is not just about external actions but also about internal attitudes and desires. As Richard Lovelace describes it, sin is "an organic network of compulsive attitudes, beliefs, and behavior deeply rooted in our alienation from God." Each day presents opportunities to uncover these hidden patterns within ourselves and bring them into the light through repentance.

This process involves:

1. **Realization**: Acknowledging specific areas where we have fallen short.

2. **Confession**: Bringing those shortcomings before God with honesty.

3. **Commitment**: Resolving to turn away from sin and pursue righteousness.

By embracing this cycle daily, we allow God's grace to continually shape us into better versions of ourselves.

Why Daily Repentance Matters

1. It Keeps Us Spiritually Grounded

Daily repentance reminds us of our dependence on God's mercy and grace. Without regular self-examination, it becomes easy to grow complacent or prideful in our spiritual journey. Repentance keeps us humble by confronting us with the reality of our need for forgiveness.

As James 4:6 states, "God opposes the proud but gives grace to the humble." Through daily repentance, we maintain a posture of humility that opens us up to receive God's transformative power.

2. It Promotes Personal Growth

Repentance is not just about addressing past mistakes; it's also about fostering growth for the future. When we take time each day to reflect on our actions and attitudes, we gain deeper self-awareness. This awareness allows us to identify negative patterns—such as anger, jealousy, or selfishness—and work toward replacing them with virtues like patience, kindness, and generosity.

The Apostle Paul emphasizes this transformative aspect in Titus 2:11-14: "For the grace of God has appeared... training us to renounce ungodliness... [and] live self-controlled, upright, and godly lives."

3. It Strengthens Our Relationships

Daily repentance not only improves our relationship with God but also enhances how we interact with others. By acknowledging our faults regularly, we become more empathetic toward others' struggles and less judgmental when they fall short.

In Matthew 7:3-5, Jesus warns against focusing on others' flaws while ignoring our own shortcomings. Daily introspection helps us remove the metaphorical "plank" from our eyes so that we can approach others with compassion rather than criticism.

Practical Steps for Incorporating Daily Repentance

1. Set Aside Time for Reflection

Carve out a specific time each day—whether in the morning or evening—to reflect on your thoughts, words, and actions. Ask yourself questions like:

- Did I honor God in my decisions today?

- Were there moments when I acted out of selfishness or pride?

- How can I do better tomorrow?

Journaling these reflections can help you track your progress over time.

2. Confess Your Sins Honestly

Confession is an essential part of repentance. In prayer or quiet meditation, bring your sins before God without minimizing or justifying them. As 1 John 1:9 assures us: "If we confess our sins, He is faithful and just to forgive us."

You may also consider confessing certain struggles to a

trusted friend or mentor who can provide accountability and encouragement (James 5:16).

3. Seek Forgiveness from Others

If your actions have hurt someone else, take steps to make amends by apologizing sincerely and seeking their forgiveness. This act not only restores relationships but also reinforces your commitment to living righteously.

4. Focus on Specific Changes

Rather than making vague resolutions like "I'll try harder," identify concrete steps you can take to address specific areas of weakness—for example:

- If you struggle with impatience during stressful situations at work or home, practice mindfulness techniques.

- If gossip has been an issue for you recently, commit to speaking positively about others instead.

Small changes made consistently over time lead to significant transformation.

The Joyful Outcome of Daily Repentance

While repentance may initially seem daunting or uncomfortable due to its focus on confronting sinfulness head-on—it ultimately leads to joy and freedom! Through daily repentance:

- We experience peace by releasing guilt and shame.

- We grow closer to God as His love renews us.

- We become instruments of His grace in the lives around us.

As Hosea 14 beautifully illustrates: when Israel turned back toward God after acknowledging their sins sincerely—they were met not with condemnation but healing love (Hosea 14:4). Similarly today—our genuine efforts at turning back toward Him are met abundantly by His mercy!

Conclusion: A Lifelong Journey

Daily repentance isn't about achieving perfection overnight; rather—it's about committing ourselves anew every single day toward becoming more Christ-like individuals who reflect His love & light wherever they go!

Let this chapter serve both encouragement & challenge—to embrace *repenting* wholeheartedly—not merely occasional ritual—but vibrant lifestyle filled hope renewal redemption!

Chapter 8: The Fruits of Repentance

Repentance is not merely an act of turning away from sin; it is a transformative journey that leads to a life filled with peace, joy, and spiritual growth. True repentance brings us into alignment with God's will, allowing His Spirit to work within us and produce the fruits of the Spirit as described in Galatians 5:22-23. These fruits—love, joy, peace, patience, kindness, goodness, faithfulness, gentleness, and self-control—are the evidence of a life transformed by God's grace. In this chapter, we will explore how repentance opens the door to these spiritual blessings and transforms every aspect of our lives.

The Transformative Power of Repentance

Repentance begins with acknowledging our sins and turning away from them. This act of humility allows us to receive God's forgiveness and experience His grace. But repentance does not stop at confession—it initiates a process of transformation. When we repent sincerely, we invite the Holy Spirit to dwell within us and begin His sanctifying work.

The Apostle Paul emphasizes this transformation in Galatians 5:16-25. He contrasts the "acts of the flesh"—such as hatred, jealousy, selfish ambition—with the "fruit of the Spirit." The acts of the flesh represent a life dominated by sin and separation from God. In contrast, the fruit of the Spirit reflects a life that has been renewed through repentance and submission to God's will.

When we repent and walk by the Spirit (Galatians 5:16), we are no longer controlled by sinful desires but are empowered to live according to God's design. This transformation is not instantaneous but occurs gradually as we grow in faith and obedience.

Peace With God

One of the most profound outcomes of repentance is peace with God. Before repentance, sin creates a barrier between us and our Creator (Isaiah 59:2). However, when we turn back to Him in humility and faith, that barrier is removed. Romans 5:1 declares, "Therefore, since we have been justified through faith, we have peace with God through our Lord Jesus Christ."

This peace is not merely an absence of conflict; it is a deep sense of harmony with God's purposes for our lives. It allows us to rest in His sovereignty even amid trials and uncertainties. As Paul writes in Philippians 4:7, "The peace of God, which transcends all understanding," guards our hearts and minds in Christ Jesus.

Personal Growth Through Spiritual Fruit

Repentance sets us on a path toward personal growth as we begin to bear spiritual fruit. Each fruit listed in Galatians 5:22-23 represents an area where God works within us to make us more like Christ:

Love

Repentance enables us to love others selflessly because it frees us from pride and selfishness. As recipients of God's unconditional love (1 John 4:19), we are empowered to extend that same love to others—even those who may have wronged us.

Joy

True joy flows from knowing that our sins are forgiven and that we are reconciled with God (Psalm 51:12). This joy is not dependent on external circumstances but arises from an inner confidence in God's goodness and promises.

Peace

As mentioned earlier, peace with God leads to inner tranquility. This peace also extends outwardly as we become peacemakers in our relationships (Matthew 5:9).

Patience

Repentance teaches us patience by reminding us of God's patience toward us (2 Peter 3:9). As we grow in this virtue, we learn to endure difficulties without losing hope or becoming bitter.

Kindness

A repentant heart overflows with kindness because it recognizes how much kindness has been shown by God (Ephesians 4:32). This fruit manifests in acts of compassion toward others.

Goodness

Goodness reflects moral integrity—a desire to do what is right according to God's standards. Repentance aligns our hearts with His righteousness so that goodness becomes a natural outflow.

Faithfulness

Through repentance, we develop greater trust in God's faithfulness toward us (Lamentations 3:22-23). In turn, this inspires loyalty and reliability in our relationships with others.

Gentleness

Gentleness stems from humility—a key component of repentance. It allows us to approach others with grace rather than harshness or judgment (Colossians 3:12).

Self-Control

Finally, self-control is cultivated as we surrender our desires to God's authority (Titus 2:11-12). Repentance helps break the power of sinful habits so that we can live disciplined lives for His glory.

Write the Conclusion

**The Fruits of Repentance are not merely ideals or abstract concepts; they are tangible evidence of a life transformed by God's grace. When we repent sincerely—turning away from sin and toward God—we open ourselves to His sanctifying work through the Holy Spirit. This transformation is beautifully captured in Galatians 5:22-23, where Paul describes the fruits of the Spirit as love, joy, peace, patience, kindness, goodness, faithfulness, gentleness, and self-control. These qualities are not achieved through human effort but are cultivated by abiding in Christ and walking in step with His Spirit.

Repentance brings peace with God—a reconciliation that fills our hearts with joy and assurance. It fosters personal growth as we shed old habits and embrace new ones aligned with God's will. Relationships once fractured by sin can be restored through humility and forgiveness born out of true repentance. And perhaps most profoundly, repentance leads us into a life marked by greater joy—not fleeting happiness tied to circumstances but deep-seated contentment rooted in God's unchanging love.

As you reflect on this journey of repentance and renewal, remember that it is an ongoing process—a daily surrender to God's will and a commitment to grow in Christlikeness. The fruits of repentance are not only blessings for your own life but also testimonies that glorify God and draw others closer to Him.

So take heart! Repentance is not something to fear or avoid; it is a gift that opens the door to abundant life in Christ. As you walk this path of transformation, may you experience the fullness of God's grace and bear fruit that lasts for eternity. Let your life be a living testament to the power of repentance—a beacon pointing others toward the hope found in Jesus Christ alone.

Conclusion

The Call to Repentance: A Lifelong Journey Toward God

In closing, let us remember that repentance is not merely an event but a divine invitation into a transformed life—a journey marked by humility, surrender, and hope. From Genesis to Revelation, Scripture resounds with this call to turn from sin and turn toward God. It is not just about feeling sorrow for wrongdoing but about aligning our hearts with God›s will through faith in Jesus Christ.

Repentance begins with recognizing our sinfulness before a holy God. As John the Baptist declared, "Repent, for the kingdom of heaven is at hand" (Matthew 3:2), so too are we called to acknowledge our need for forgiveness and restoration. Yet repentance does not end there—it demands action. True repentance bears fruit in our lives as we walk in obedience to God's commands (Matthew 3:8). This transformation reflects not only a change of behavior but also a change of heart—a reorientation of our entire being toward God.

Moreover, repentance is not confined to the moment of salvation; it is an ongoing practice for every believer. Daily we are called to examine ourselves before God, confess our sins, and seek His grace anew (1 John 1:9). As Thomas Watson aptly described it, "Repentance unto life" involves grief over sin coupled with joy in God's mercy—a turning away from sin with full purpose of new obedience.

Yet even as we strive toward holiness through repentance, let us never forget that it is ultimately God's kindness that leads us there (Romans 2:4). The gospel assures us that no matter how far we have strayed or how deeply we have fallen into sin, God's grace abounds all the more for those who repent and believe (Luke 15:7). In this truth lies our greatest hope—that through Jesus Christ's sacrifice on the cross, forgiveness has been secured once and for all.

As you close this book on repentance, may you be inspired not only to reflect on your own need for transformation but also to share this message with others. The Great Commission compels us to proclaim both "repentance toward God" and "faith toward our Lord Jesus Christ" (Acts 20:21). In doing so, we participate in God's redemptive work—calling others out of darkness into His marvelous light.

So today—and every day—heed Christ's words afresh: "Repent!" Let them echo in your heart as both commandment and invitation. Turn from sin; turn toward Him who loves you with an everlasting love; walk forward in faith bearing fruits worthy of repentance until He returns or calls you home.

May your life be marked by continual surrender to God's will through heartfelt repentance—a testimony of His transforming power at work within you—and may you find joy unspeakable as you abide ever closer to Him who alone makes all things new.

About Apostle Bill Amor

Apostle Bill Amor's life is a testament to the power of faith, perseverance, and divine intervention. Diagnosed with autism as a child and considered high-functioning as an adult, Apostle Amor has faced challenges that would have broken many. His journey from despair to spiritual awakening forms the foundation of his new book, Repent, which seeks to inspire readers to find hope and redemption through God.

Born into a world that often misunderstood him, young Bill struggled with feelings of isolation and inadequacy. Despite these challenges, he displayed remarkable determination. At the age of 12, he achieved a significant milestone by winning a reading competition—an accomplishment that filled him with pride and optimism. However, this joy was short-lived when his mother tearfully shared devastating news from the doctor: he was not expected to live beyond the age of 28 to 32.

This revelation shattered his world. Overwhelmed by fear and hopelessness, Bill sought solace in his best friend John Straw, only to discover that John had been taken away by his brother Andy. Feeling abandoned and consumed by anger, he fled into the woods near his home. It was there, amidst the trees and shadows of doubt, that he cried out to God in desperation.

Bill's life changed forever on that fateful day. As he climbed a steep hill toward his neighbor's house, he encountered what can only be described as a divine vision: Jesus Christ Himself appeared before him at the top of the hill near a chain-link fence. The image was vivid—Jesus stood before him with pockmarks where His beard had been removed and glistening divots on His cheeks and chin. He did not resemble traditional depictions; instead, He appeared timeless yet distinct from modern trends.

This miraculous encounter marked the beginning of Apostle Amor's transformation. From a young boy who felt lost and unworthy, he grew into a man devoted to spreading God's message of love and repentance. Through trials and tribulations—including struggles with literacy—he found strength in faith and discovered his purpose as an apostle.

In Repent, Apostle Bill Amor shares his deeply personal story alongside powerful lessons about redemption, forgiveness, and unwavering trust in God's plan. His journey serves as an inspiration for anyone grappling with doubt or seeking meaning in their lives.

Apostle Amor's mission is clear: to guide others toward spiritual healing by sharing his testimony of divine grace. With humility born from hardship and wisdom gained through faith, he invites readers to embark on their own journeys toward repentance and renewal.